Etch the Line Around my Never Ending Heart

Jewel Winkler

Presentation by *BookLeaf Publishing*

Web: www.bookleafpub.com

E-mail: info@bookleafpub.com

ISBN: 9789357613170

First edition 2022

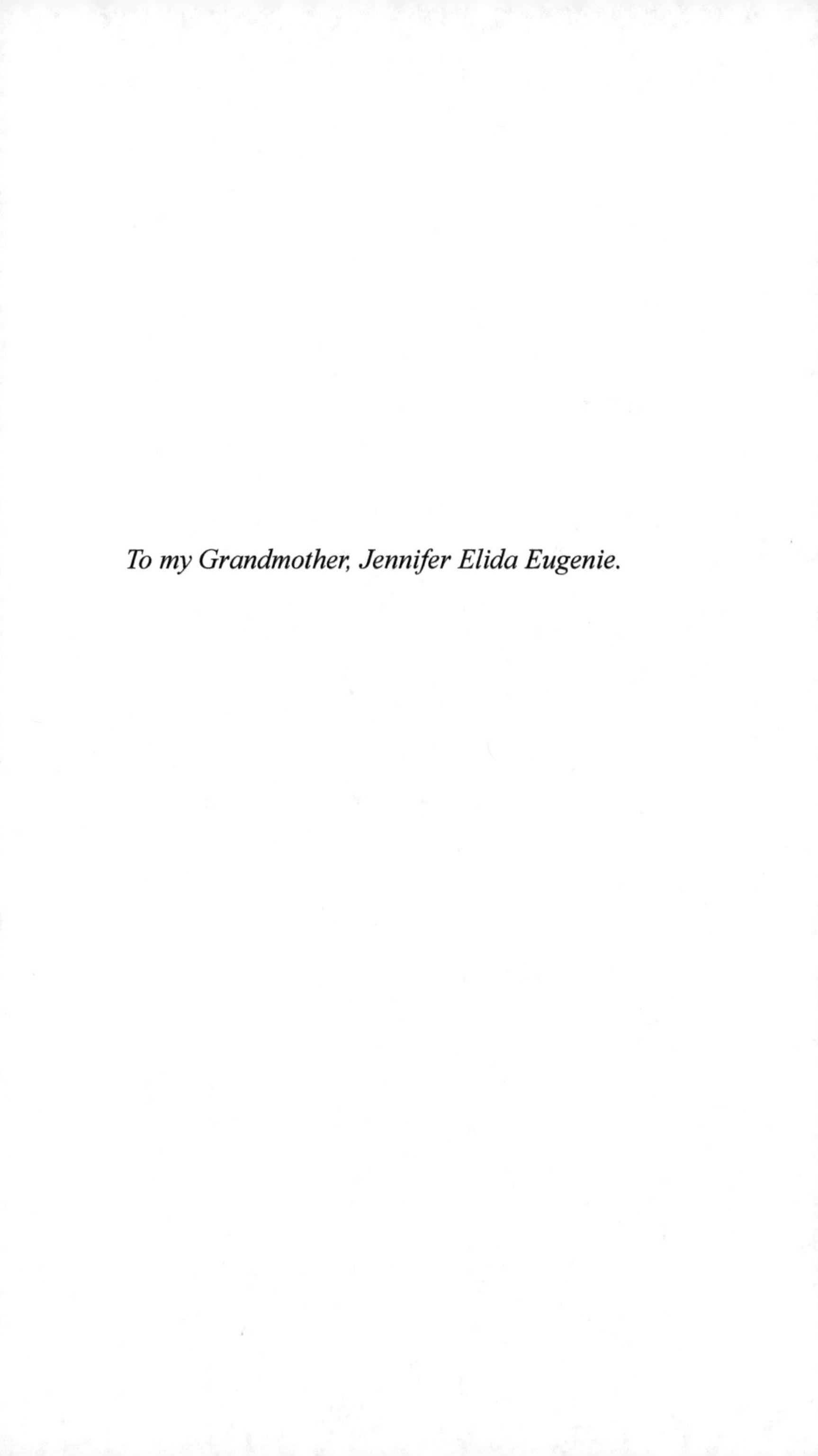

To my Grandmother, Jennifer Elida Eugenie.

ACKNOWLEDGEMENT

It is imperative that I acknowledge all the love I have found (or the love that has found me) in our Little Flower Shop. Kirsten, Natalie, Jule and Miae.

To Little Girls.
To Little Rivers making Big Streams.
To Honouring Our Creativity and Dreams.

And of course, to the love I was holding out for, Anthony Rowley.

Etch the Line Around my Never Ending Heart

Etch the line around my never ending heart.

I reject you dying.
I so long to live.
I am.
I am living.

Little girl in me says
Watch me.
Mama.
While you curl. Ever inward.
To a place I dare not reach.

I call out to you.
I hold my heart out to you.
I throw myself.
Nearly. Everywhere.
Except.
Oblivion.
I can't.
I can't go there with you.

I call out to you.
There is no sound. No movement.

I hold my light in your dark.

I love you
I love you
I love you.

Etch the line around my never ending heart.

In Your Eyes

Husband and I did not know what to do with my
son.
My grown son.
He was drowning.
Will I always be a witness to the water?

And my daughter. So like me.
She moved around the kitchen. Swift. Efficient.
Making it livable for me. For her too.

Why am I so tired today? I wonder if I will ever
feel like her.
An aliveness there. I used to know. I watch her.
Like a mirror to the past. Another version of me.
But. Not me.
And husband. What did he think?
I watch him pour too much sugar in his coffee.
My daughter's eyes.
Diabetes.
Heart. Attack.
Unwell parents.
Flashes of concern settle in her gaze. But she
says nothing. Today.

It all happened so fast. The shock.

My son. So like my first husband. His father.
The yelling.
The explosions.
The anger.
You did not know where it lived. Whence it
came.

No wonder my daughter cannot take him.
So like me.
She'd cut that cord if she could.
She knew they weren't made of the same things.
It never mattered. It still does not matter.
But it's there. Plain as day.

I watched how gracefully she threw her cup of
warm coffee on my son.
It was like watching an Olympian shot put to
perfection.
A magnificent defense.

My son sputtered like a child.
Wanting to be violent.
He opted for viciously swiping wet coffee from
his hair.
Pathetically, flicking it, in her direction.
Not quite like his dad.
Might not hit her.

My husband laughed hysterically. Awkwardly.
Shocked.
I clutched my head. Tension.
My body shaking from the stress.

My daughter silently asking us. Her parents.
How did we let it get this far?
Heart. Broken.
She is always holding the bag.

I could not look at her.
Because I did not know.

Talking to Photographs

I light candles
Bring flowers
A little altar with your photograph
I talk to your picture for a while
Praying
Praying, also, that you hear me.

THUNK

An astounding warmth rushes into the center of
me
Filling me
You must hear me.
I nearly cry.

I must have dialed the right number to your
heaven
Where you house my passed away puppies and
unborn children.
And you like the painting I live in
My honey fields and wild flowers
Tumbling blue sky and cotton clouds.
That big white barn that unites earth and my
heaven.

I tell you about my boyfriend and his dog.
My mom.
I ask for help.
Divinity.
I let only a few tears go

Even though I long to cry for hours
Losing myself to images in the stippled ceiling
as my tears dry
A serene calm washing over me
The salt tightening over the apples of my cheeks
The closest I'll get to an ocean for now.

I forget my body and look for messages in the
ceiling
A sign.

I imagine stars, the way you lose yourself in
those too.
And cool night air over my face.
Waking me up and lulling me to sleep.
I swing in my hammock while the candles burn
down.

whispers
I pray.
I say thank you.
I pray.
Thank you.

Pray.
Thank you.
Pray.

My praying becomes my thanking.
My thanking – my praying.

Honey Bungalow

I fold in the gold like honey
Anyway I can
I wrap you around me
I create a little house, a bungalow
In your heart
I pour the liquid carefully
Filling every crack.

We exchange photographs, yellow calcite and
light
Like sweet tokens of honey comb
Little memories
Little boy with soft blonde hair
Little girl with gold-red tendrils
I adore these memories
These stories
My cup, our cup – is so full.

I fold in the gold of my Spirit
So I may be layered with a rich, warm and
honeyed heart
Into you.

I dream of a little yellow house.
I remember who I am.

Patience & Healing

I don't know where I begin or end
I don't know where to flow
And I used to do it so well.
I want to go.

Ardent emotions hover somewhere beneath my
skin, others more deeply sit.
They take turns bouncing below the surface,
rising and settling, like the bones of an old
house.
I long for them to burst. From my pores like
flowers. And never die.
Love in a mist.

But they stay stubbornly beneath the layers.
Regenerating for an eternity.
My tired heart,
Beating.

To surrender.
To surrender? Throat catches, a head shake.
To surrender this heart.
The hardest.
Love in a mist.

I long for a touch so warm; a love so golden, so
great.

My world somehow balanced.
Leaving me uneven.

Temperance.

Table

I sat for hours at the table.
Waiting for my heart to stop.
But it didn't.

I traced the wood and all its lines, hearts, rings
and rough marks.
I got lost in it's art.
Letting the wood take my quiet little storms.

When did I become this?
I talked it all out.

This table held me up.

Stay Soft

Stay soft? I whispered.
Stay. Soft.
How, I asked out loud.
Do I stay this way?

When they question your beauty.
Your reasons.
Your dreams.
You must walk away.

You must stay soft.
So a mold does not take.

Stay soft. I whispered.
Stay soft.

Naïveté -"4. not having previously been the
subject of a scientific experiment, as an animal."

Shaman Woman, Nokomis

14

She dances and shuffles around me,
Moon Daughter, Grandmother.

She slaps me with her feathers.
My heart lifts in slows breaths.
Musky sage settling on my skin.

Your heart is closed, honey.
She says to me.
Not broken?
No, she says with a playful smile.
{grandmother}
No? I ask, smile growing, eyes full.
She slaps me with her feathers some more.

Come in, Kjæreste

Wake me in the night
Wake me in the early morn
A simple touch
I will know

You wish to be let in
Come in
I say
My body unfolds from its natural ways

Let me embrace your soul
In every way
Let me wrap myself around you
Let my warmth envelope you

Come in my darling
Come in, rock it out with me
That maddening soul
Come in

Come in, my beloved
Breathe into me
You soul may stay
Come in, my Kjæreste

Her Name Means Rain

She takes my hand and holds it to her face
Her cheeks plump and warm
She presses my hand there
Finding a perfect mould to my bones
She is my little love
My heart flutters and cracks
A whole world in my palm.

It rains gently there and reigns in beauty.

{To my niece, Amarynn}

Living in the Glow

Unfold into you
Into me
Holy heaven, I need a good one. I pray.
It was you, it was you all along.

I see your eyes, you see mine.
You say they are warm like the sun.
Your blues, as big as the sky.
Your touch.
Is a balm.
I reached out and you reached back.
Spark. Click. Bang.
Quiet.
The Moment.
Your eyes dazzled at me.
I always said goodbye, wondering if we would
say hello.
Again.

Paper heart in my dreams.
I couldn't see then, but you.
You gave it to me.
I am a wave, I say.
You say, wash over me.
Falling.

Falling quickly.

You touch your chest when you speak.
When you tell stories, where your heart beats.
Where your lungs breathe.
I imagine living there. Asking you endless
questions about your Sisu.
Let it unfold.
Let it open.
Let the gold rush in.
I don't see you for a week.
But we talk on the phone.
Lifeline.
I trace my heart line.
Are you my new home. All this time.

I smile. I look at you.
I look at Gruff.
Ruff. Ruff. Ruff.
I see a home.
I see so much.
Let it unfold, I whisper.
Let him catch up.
My King of Cups.

I live here now.
I live in our glow.

These Bones

May these bones love you.
May these bones be evidence of my warm soul.
Of this tired soul.
Of this soul that has been worn again and again.

May these bones keep a story.
For all stories come from somewhere.

And may it be these bones.

Leaving

Some of the break up is real fuzzy. I can clearly remember some of the words said but most of it felt like a big smear. To be honest, it was like I was out of my body the entire time it was happening. And I was watching myself on a screen. And the better version of me was watching it all play out. My chest like an egg, cracked open and spilling into a sickly mess on the floor. Some of me was still holding firm to the membrane but most of me slipping away from myself. I made no move to intervene. That other version of me, kept my eyes wide open. Leading me out the door, lined with light. Pushing me below my shoulders, straightening out my slumped back. Ground beneath me moved. When I finally caught up with myself. I wondered what it truly was that I had left behind.

Heart Strings

I think I spend much of my time up in my head.
And I imagine these little strings that run from
the corners of my mind.
All the way down to my heart.

They run along my neck, my throat, weaving
through the muscle and the bone.
Tugging and catching in areas I can't see.
But I feel them, like a strange pully system.
They are made of strung gold, thin and worn
from strain.
Trying to hold the weight.

Evidence in My Bones

My bones are stiff from not loving.
My bones ache from not being embraced.

My insides are heavy but my mind is weightless
and floating around.
My feet touch the ground and yet the roots don't
take.

The words I say are soundless.
Nothing leaves me breathless.

Because I am living.
But I am not loving.

Still Healing

23

I would sit very still. Given tool, in hand.
Cerebral in state.
And wonder when the magic within me would
resurface again.
I knew it lingered yet, somewhere, deep within
my bones.
Where all magic comes from.

It made me shiver. It made me ache.
But my paper, my canvas, my mind,
remained blank.

Bed

A lovely place where the pillows meet.
Where my head sinks in, awaiting the infamous
sleep.

I think a bed is where two souls should meet.
But really, it is just me.
In the awful in between.
Nothing to my day.
Just the silence, a slight ruffle of my feet.
Laying, wondering. If you or I will ever meet.
In the lovely place where the pillows sleep.

I ache to fill the space.
In my heart.
In my head.
This lovely place in my bed.
Where the pillows meet.
Where dreams find me in sleep.

Generations

25

May your art.
Be my art too.
I want to honour your legacy.
I want to continue your beauty.
Forever and always,
Because I love you and this body,
Demands it of me.